Guardian of the ...

The Story of Newark Castle

PAMELA MARSHALL
&
JOHN SAMUELS

1. Mid 19th-century watercolour of the cattle market at Newark Castle (artist unknown)

CONTENTS

	Introduction	3
1.	In the Beginning	5
2.	The Coming of the Normans	10
3.	Alexander the Magnificent and the 12th-Century Castle	13
4.	King John at Newark Castle	31
5.	The Early 14th Century Castle	32
6.	The Castle in the 15th, 16th and early 17th Centuries	37
7.	1646 and After	40
	Glossary	42
	Further Reading	44

© Newark Castle Trust 1997

ISBN 0 900943 95 5

2. The riverside front of Newark Castle viewed from the bridge

Introduction

The visitor entering Newark from the west and crossing the bridge over the River Trent comes across an impressive sight. The riverside front of Newark Castle, standing almost to its battlements and one of the longest in Britain, is among the most spectacular views in the county. From the bridge we can still appreciate the magnificence of the 12th-century gatehouse. Three storeys high, it remains the most complete example of a Romanesque gatehouse to survive in England.

Yet less than twenty per cent of the medieval castle still stands, even in ruins. In 1646 it was deliberately destroyed on the orders of Parliament after Newark had surrendered to Roundhead forces after a long siege. It was a symbolic act. Since the Norman Conquest in 1066 castles had represented the power of the ruling classes. They had been the 'secret weapon' of William the Conqueror. Quickly built by forced labour using earth and timber, they formed the bases from which the relatively small Norman occupation forces were rapidly able to extend their hold on newly taken territory. As Norman rule was established, they were improved and often rebuilt in stone. Castles became complicated. In times of war or civil unrest they had to be strongholds, although in practice these circumstances did not arise very often in the history of most castles. The nobility governed the lands in their charge, so castles had to be centres of administration and of justice. Taxes would be collected there, courts would be held and prisoners would be kept in dungeons pending trial. The nobility held their place in society by their ability to fight, raise and lead armies, protect the possessions of their king and their own people and keep the peace in their own territory. Their castles were the visible mark of a regime whose power was based on military strength. But, the castle was also a home to its lord, though usually one of many, and in time a greater accent on comfort crept in. Castles had to fulfil many functions, not least of which was to make a visible show of power. The prestige of the lord would be proclaimed to all in the outward appearance of his building.

How do we know?

Research on Newark Castle has been carried out over a period of forty years, each fragment of evidence helping to piece together a picture of how the building looked and functioned. Over the past five years this picture has begun to gel together. With the financial help of Newark and Sherwood District Council and many other sponsors, investigations have been carried out on two fronts. A programme of research excavations by Newark Castle Trust have taken place in the castle grounds. Archaeological recording and observation of the ruins has also been possible, sponsored by English Heritage, and carried out by Trent and Peak Archaeological Trust. As decayed stone and Victorian tarmac was removed so that the fabric could be consolidated and made safe, much information about the medieval building was revealed.

3. *The gatehouse*

Using this information along with that from earlier investigations, we can now see that all the roles expected of a medieval castle were played at Newark. This book will try to explain them. Technical words printed in italics are explained in a glossary at the back of the book.

Acknowledgements

Although this book is the result of the collaborative efforts of the two named authors, it has benefited from the researches of many others. Should the reader wish to explore the subject in more detail, information about useful publications is provided in the final section on further reading.

The present study would not have been possible without the support, encouragement and advice of several organisations and individuals. In particular we would like to acknowledge Newark Castle Trust, Newark and Sherwood District Council, Newark Town Council, Nottinghamshire County Council, Trent and Peak Archaeological Trust and English Heritage. A number of local and national charities, local businesses, individuals and especially Thomas Fish and Sons, the Nottingham builders, contributed to the work undertaken by Newark Castle Trust. Glyn Jones FRPS provided many of the photographs taken during the excavations and David Taylor produced the drawings and spectacular reconstructions commissioned by Newark and Sherwood District Council. Roy Wells, Dave Bower, the Newark Advertiser, Newark Museum, Newark Library and the City of Lincoln Archaeology Unit have allowed the use of their collections of illustrations. Newark Castle Trust, Newark and Sherwood District Council and English Heritage have allowed us to use information and illustrations from various projects connected with the castle. We owe a debt of gratitude to the many individuals who gave up their own time to assist with surveys and excavations in recent years; without the excavations in particular this account would have been the poorer. Finally, our special thanks to Rupert Vinnicombe, Newark District librarian and Ian Brown, of Nottinghamshire County Council's Leisure Services Department, for organising this publication and ensuring its appearance.

4. Excavations in Area 3

5. Consolidation work being carried out on the castle fabric

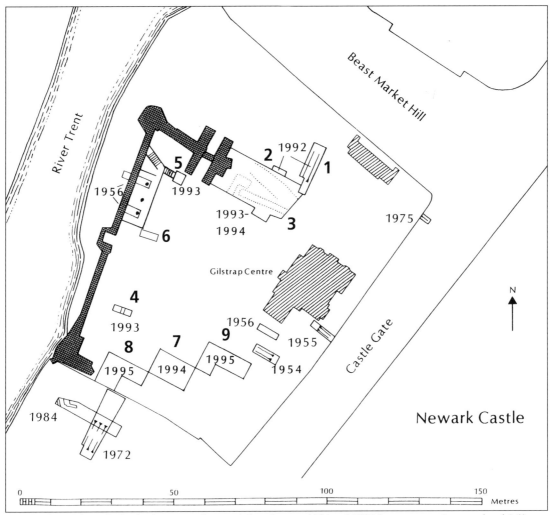

6. Plan of the castle site showing excavations carried out between 1954 and 1995 (recent excavations numbered 1-9)

1. In the Beginning

The castle is sited on a river cliff on the east bank of the River Trent which is now canalised. In earlier times the river was prone to flooding and the land to the west was marshy. The site was ideal as it would be safe from flood water but at the same time protected by it. Also, the land falls away on both the north and south sides, making it easy to defend. The town stands to the east, where the slope is more gradual. Not surprisingly, the position was occupied well before the Middle Ages. Two seasons of excavation on the north side of the castle grounds, marked Area 3 on illus. 6 revealed less than expected about the castle because many archaeological layers had been removed in the 19th century. However, the deeper archaeological levels investigated here showed more about the pre-castle history of the site. The presence of Bronze Age pottery, flint tools and an Iron Age coin suggests occupation from an early date. A great deal of Roman pottery and some artefacts were found, enough to show that there was Roman settlement of some kind, but later activities had destroyed any clear pattern of structures. Only two ditches, marked 276 and 373 on illus. 7, could be identified as dating from the Roman period.

5th to late 9th Centuries
More evidence remained of early Saxon occupation. A very large, curving ditch bounded the north side of the site, marked 287 on illus. 7. This was filled with animal bones and early to mid-Saxon pottery, showing it had been used as a refuse tip. The pottery from the lower levels was very similar to burial urns from a pagan Saxon

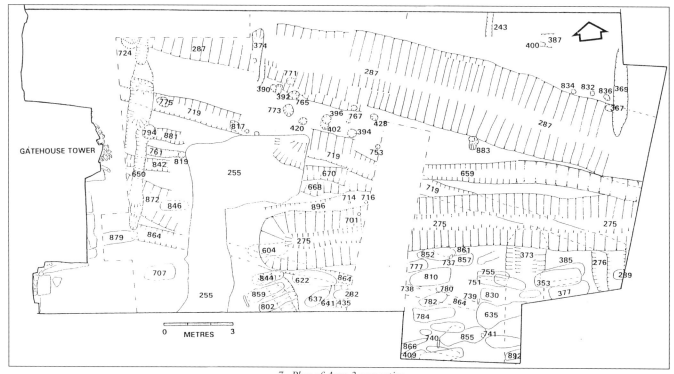

7. Plan of Area 3 excavation

cemetery at the southern end of Mill Gate. The ditch also contained *loom-weights* and a pair of copper alloy tweezers. Again, no firm information about buildings belonging to this occupation was recovered, although a shallow hollow, marked 243 on illus. 7, was of the same date and is likely to be the remains of a timber beam which formed the base of a wattle wall.

9th to mid-11th Centuries

Excavating on the east side of the site between 1954 and 1956, Professor Maurice Barley and Freda Waters found the traces of late Saxon occupation (illus. 6). Along with charcoal, wood ash, animal bone and pottery sherds, they recovered the foundations of a house which had been destroyed when the *rampart*, or defensive bank of the castle, was raised. In Area 7 a line of stones marking another foundation was discovered in 1994, which might also belong to the Saxon settlement (illus. 8). Excavations in 1992 in Area 1 found several post-holes containing 10th century pottery, sealed by what was left of the castle bank raised on top of them. Although the structures of this period have proved elusive, the people themselves are more in evidence, for their burial ground came to light in Area 3.

Saxon Cemetery

The cemetery was Christian, for the graves were orientated east-west and there were no *grave goods*.

8. Stone foundation found in Area 7, 1994

7

Some of the bodies were laid straight in the ground; others had been put into 'coffins' made up of flat slabs of stone pieced together, called *cists*. Others had boxes of stone slabs only around their heads. Six of the graves were marked with roughly shaped rectangles of stone stood on end. *Radio carbon dating* of skeletons showed that the cemetery had been in use for a least a century, from c.950 to c.1070. Many of the graves had been disturbed by others cut into them at a later date. Over 50 individual graves were found in Area 3 containing 20 children and 31 adults, roughly equally divided between the sexes. Two further graves were found whilst excavating Area 5 and it was clear that the graveyard had covered a large area. The fact that it was reported in the 1830s that 100 burials were disturbed while land next to the gatehouse was being cleared to make a cattle market tends to confirm this.

The Saxon Settlement

It is known that the Medieval defences of Newark formed a fairly regular rectangle, following Lombard Street, Carter Gate and Appleton Gate, then Slaughterhouse Lane and the west side of Castle Gate (illus. 11). It has been assumed that these defences were first set out in the 9th century against Viking raids and that the Saxon borough lay within these boundaries. However, excavations on

9. Recording the late Saxon cemetery in Area 3

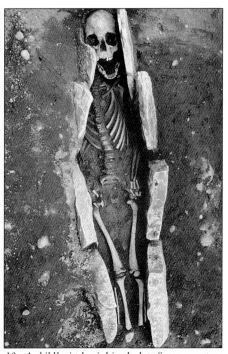

10. A child's cist burial in the late Saxon cemetery in Area 3

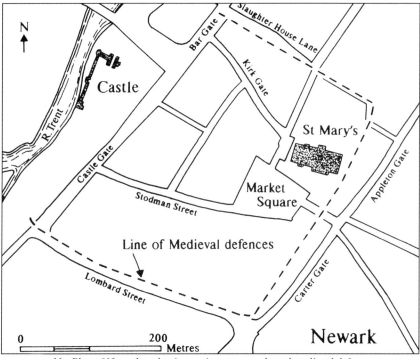

11. Plan of Newark to showing main streets, castle and medieval defences

the defences carried out by Malcolm Todd in the 1970s in Lombard Street, Mount Lane, Castle Gate and the Old White Hart Yard produced no evidence of Saxon activity. He concluded that the Saxon borough occupied a much smaller area within the town and that the defences had been created along with the castle. At that time the castle was thought to date from about 1130. Excavations in Slaughterhouse Lane in 1988 seemed to show that the town rampart here pre-dated the castle on the evidence of pottery earlier than the 12th century. However, this pottery could mean that the rampart is contemporary with the castle, which is now known to have been built just after the Norman invasion.

The regular shape of the medieval town as defined by the defensive line is rather at odds with the less regular shape formed by Kirk Gate and Stodman Street and it may be that the area enclosed by these, with the market square on the east and the castle on the west, represents the Saxon borough. There have been many excavations outside this enclave but they have produced no proof of Saxon occupation at all. There has been no excavation inside except on the castle site, which has proved that Saxon activity here was very concentrated. In 1994 a *watching brief* in the Co-operative building in Kirk Gate, just within the proposed Saxon boundary, also observed the site of a Saxon pottery kiln. Further excavation within the town would obviously help to clear up this question, but it looks increasingly as if Newark was developed as a planned town by the Normans, encapsulating the existing, but smaller, Saxon settlement within it.

12. *Newark from the air. The nucleus of the Saxon town probably lay within the triangle formed by Kirk Gate, Stodman Street and the river*

2. The Coming of the Normans

Before excavations by Newark Castle Trust took place it was thought that the first castle at Newark was built about 1130. It was known that the bishops of Lincoln were created lords of the manor shortly after the Norman Conquest and that they had a house on the site, but evidence recovered since 1993 shows that this was much more than a manor house.

The late Saxon cemetery was disturbed by the creation of a ditch, marked 275 on illus. 7, which cut along its northern edge. The ditch was V-shaped with a square bottom and the profile of its steep sides remained so sharp it must have been fairly rapidly filled in. Pottery dated it to the middle of the 11th century, about the time of the Norman Conquest. The west end of the ditch ended abruptly, cutting a grave in two. Shortly afterwards the whole

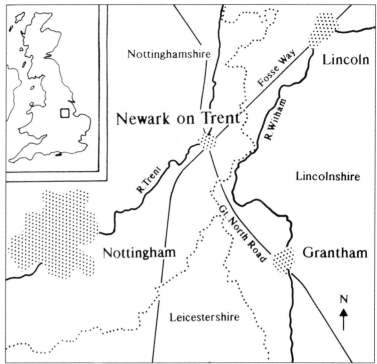

13. Sketch map showing Newark's geographical location and river and road routes

of Area 3 was covered by a massive earth bank or *rampart* built of red clay which had been dug out of a *moat* further north. This marks the coming of the first castle. Ditch 275 seems to represent the means of support for a *palisade*, or timber wall, with a gate at its west end. Its date almost certainly links it with the Norman invasion. Perhaps it was dug by the people of Newark against the invader: more likely it was built by Normans when they first took the town, to be rapidly replaced by a more substantial earth and timber castle.

The First Castle

The first castle at Newark may well have been built in the wake of William the Conqueror's push into northern territory during the winter of 1068-9. Having built two castles at York, the Anglo-Saxon Chronicle tells us that he went on to establish castles at Nottingham, Lincoln and 'elsewhere in those parts'. Research has shown that William concentrated his castle building programme on existing centres of population and administration. There was considerable advantage in controlling Lincoln, which was a very large and well established inland port of Roman origin with international trading links. Nottingham, although much smaller, was regarded as the head of its shire, stood on the route to the north and possessed a bridge over the Trent, a valuable asset. Newark's strategic position, however, was also considerable (illus. 13). About the same size as Nottingham, it probably enjoyed a similar standard of prosperity. It stood on the Fosse Way, one of the Roman roads which still formed the road transport network of the country, and there was very probably a ford over the river. It would not be surprising to find it targeted by the invaders as one of the key positions needed to establish control in the East Midlands.

The Normans chose to place their castle at Newark in the best defensible position, regardless of what was already there. It would also dominate both the river crossing and the Fosse Way, thus controlling two important routes. So the Saxon cemetery came to an abrupt end, covered by the northern *rampart* of the new castle and the house found by Barley and Waters underneath the eastern *rampart* was probably one of many which were swept away. The castle occupied more or less the same area as the existing park (illus. 14). Its western perimeter stood on top of the river cliff, and a palisade alone might have been considered sufficient defence here, with the river and marshes beyond. On the north, east and south sides the outer defence consisted of a deep, wide moat, the soil from which was used to raise high earthen banks which would have held strong walls of timber. These early defences are now barely recognisable on the ground but their

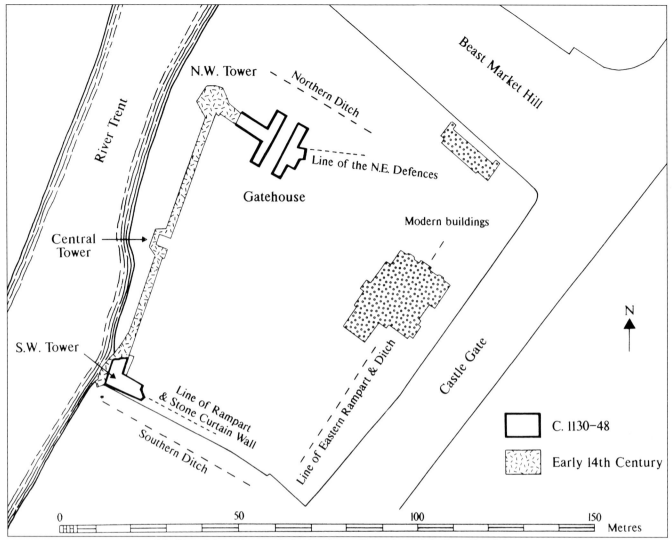

14. Plan of the castle grounds showing the standing ruins and the lines of lost defences

whereabouts has been established by various excavations (illus. 6). Their eastern line was found by Professor Barley and Freda Waters in the 1950s, although the dating evidence which was recovered never led them to question the early 12th century date which had always been given to the castle on the basis of documents. Part of the southern ditch was excavated by Terry Courtney in 1972 and again in 1984 by John Samuels, and the south rampart came to light in 1995. Excavations in Area 1 in 1992 revealed the line of the northern ditch. This had silted up during the later Middle Ages but had been re-cut as part of the 17th-century Civil War refortification of the castle.

Traces of the northern *rampart* covered the whole of the Area 3 excavation but it mostly survived only as a thin spread of clay and no finds were found to date it. Buildings had stood here during the 18th and early 19th century (illus. 15) and their demolition had been very thorough. Not even their foundations were left, and this had removed many archaeological layers. The only place where the *rampart* material survived to any depth was directly underneath a short stub of wall belonging to the 12th-century stone castle, which is still attached to the side of the gatehouse (illus. 24 and 26). The wall was built c.1130. It was 12m. tall and over 2m. thick, yet its foundations were negligible, relying largely on the hard packed clay for its stability. It was not possible to dig out any of the clay to look for dating evidence, but here it was clearly earlier than the stone wall above, and it was likely that a long time had elapsed for the clay to settle and pack down before it could have been trusted to support such a heavy load. During the 1994 and 1995 seasons of excavation, however,

11

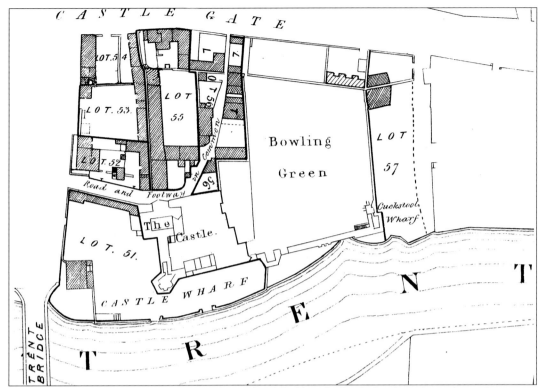

15. A plan of the castle site in 1836, showing how it had been developed after the castle was destroyed

similar *rampart* material was found to have survived to a greater depth on the south side of the site, where it was dated by pottery to the latter half of the 11th century (Areas 7, 8 and 9 on illus. 6). A bowling green had occupied this half of the castle grounds from the 18th to the late 19th centuries (illus. 15) and no damage to soil layers had been done, so the medieval archaeology survived in much better condition.

The 11th-century castle might have had a *motte*, an artificial mound of earth rising even higher than the *ramparts*, probably with a timber tower on top. When the castle was rebuilt in the 12th century the site was levelled off. The earth defences were reduced in height and a *motte* would have been thrown down at the same time. Its earlier presence would help to explain the shape of the castle plan, with its projecting north-east corner (illus. 14). The area enclosed by the *ramparts* was called the *bailey*. It would have housed several buildings: a great communal hall, kitchens, a chapel and more private apartments as well as stables, storehouses and outbuildings. The excavations have not investigated any of these, although part of a stone-flagged courtyard was revealed in Area 9 (illus. 16). After a life of about 60 years the timber buildings were no doubt very dilapidated. At this stage the castle came under the lordship of one of the most flamboyant characters of the 12th century.

16. A narrow section of a stone-flagged courtyard belonging to the 11th-century castle revealed in 1995

3. Alexander the Magnificent and the 12th-Century Castle

In 1129 the bishopric of Lincoln and its possessions came to a new incumbent. Bishop Alexander, who held the see until 1148, was to become famous throughout Christendom for his opulence, style and, in particular, for his building. Nicknamed 'the Magnificent' by the papal court, he was the natural son of Roger Bishop of Salisbury, an equally prodigious builder. His brother became Bishop of Ely. At this time high-ranking churchmen behaved and often fought much as any other nobleman. Like the rest of his family, Alexander's clerical calling was the means by which he achieved his insatiable political ambitions. His high position also gave him access to great wealth. Even so, the chronicler Henry of Huntingdon tells us that:

'Desirous of excelling every noble in his making of gifts and the splendour of his works, when his resources did not suffice for these, he was in the habit of seizing most eagerly the goods of his people . . . yet he could not succeed in this, inasmuch as he was ever squandering more and more.'

17. West front of Lincoln Cathedral (accredited to Alexander)

Shortly after Alexander's entry to the see of Lincoln, we find the first apparent reference to Newark Castle. A charter issued by Henry I around 1130, in which the wording is very ambiguous, gives permission to Bishop Alexander *that he may make a ditch and rampart of his fishpond at Newark upon the Fosse Way and that he may divert the Fosse Way through the same town as he may wish.'* This has been interpreted as permission to build the first castle. We do not know where Alexander's fishpond was, but it has been assumed that it belonged to a manor house which he was converting to a castle by adding defences, and that he wanted to divert the Fosse Way to make more room for it. In the light of archaeological research it seems clear that he had far more ambitious plans for Newark, which are entirely in keeping with his reputation. The castle which we now know already existed in 1129 would have been regarded by him as out-dated, a frontier-style fortress of the Conquest. He rebuilt and remodelled it on a lavish scale and his plans apparently extended to the whole town.

By now Newark stood on the crossroads of two main arteries of transport, the Roman Fosse Way and the Great North Road, which had developed into the main route to the north of England and Scotland (illus. 13). Alexander applied for a second royal charter giving him permission to build a bridge to carry this road across the river. For a man prominent in national politics, Newark's geographical location made it a better residential centre than Lincoln. Although he purchased land for a new bishop's palace beside his cathedral at Lincoln, he left this to his successor to build, concentrating his energies on his Newark residence. Excavations on the town defences carried out in 1972 and 1976 showed that there was also much activity on these during the second quarter of the 12th century, for which Alexander must have been responsible. The town defences formed a fairly regular rectangle, with the castle projecting slightly forward of its line on the west side and with the Fosse Way running just inside the western boundary (illus. 11). The Fosse Way at Bar Gate (widened during the 1960s) and Mill

18. Carved stones from Alexander's castle

Gate was quite narrow, but at Castle Gate widened considerably in front of the castle. As it now seems clear that the main purpose of the king's charter was to grant permission to divert the Fosse Way, perhaps it was merely to create this widening as an improvement to the town plan. A writ of Henry I of c.1133 gave Alexander permission to hold an annual fair lasting five days (18th-22nd July) and this probably took place beside the castle.

During the 1120s and 1130s it was becoming more common for stone to replace timber in castle building, but it was still very expensive. It was not unusual to build one or perhaps two of the key buildings of a castle in stone for prestige, leaving the rest in timber. Alexander's castle appears to have been largely built of stone. He built a well-planned gatehouse, at least one *angle tower* (the south-west tower), and stone *curtain walls* to replace the timber *palisades*. It was described by the chronicler, Henry of Huntingdon, as *'a magnificent castle of very ornate construction'* – in early 12th-century terms, it was 'state of the art'. A number of carved stones belonging to Alexander's castle bears out Henry of Huntingdon's description. Most of these were probably found by gardeners in the 1880s when the castle grounds were landscaped and some of them have been set into

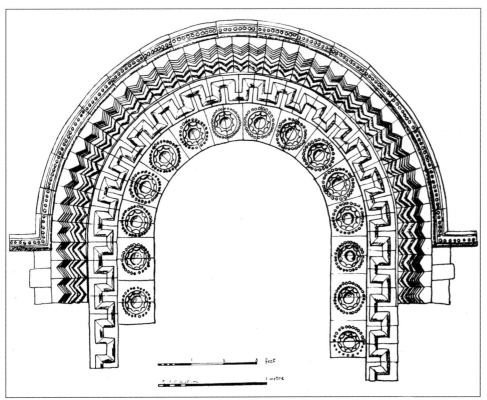

19. Drawing of 12th-century arch pieced together from carved stones found in the castle grounds

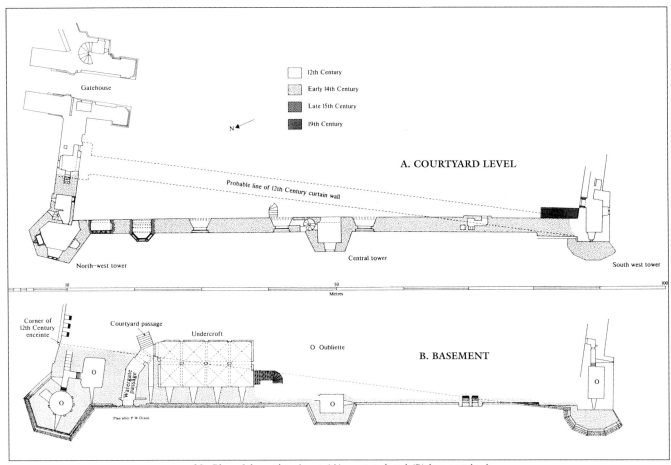

12th Century

Early 14th Century

Late 15th Century

19th Century

N

Gatehouse

A. COURTYARD LEVEL

Probable line of 12th Century curtain wall

North-west tower

Central tower

South west tower

10

50

Metres

100

Corner of 12th Century enceinte

Courtyard passage

Undercroft

O Oubliette

B. BASEMENT

Watergate Passage

O

O

O

O

O

Plan after P W Dixon

20. Plan of the castle ruins at (A) courtyard and (B) basement levels

the walls here and there (illus. 18). The largest collection of these stones came from a large and elaborate arch and they now lie in the *undercroft* beneath the present day terrace, where they have been pieced together and laid in place on a bed of sand (illus. 19). The rosette-shaped motif is quite unusual, but was also used on Malmesbury Abbey which was built by Bishop Roger of Salisbury, Alexander's father. The arch from which the building came has long gone and we cannot be sure what type of building it was. However, the elaborate decoration tells us that it was an important one, perhaps a chapel. We do know that there was a chapel of St. Philip and St. James within the castle and that it must have been quite large, for it was the scene of a society wedding in 1588 between Elizabeth Manners and William Cecil, both from important families. Alternatively, the castle might have had a stone *hall* with a decorated arched entrance, as at Durham Castle.

Only two sections of Alexander's castle remain (illus. 20). These are the gatehouse, with short stretches of wall adjoining (illus. 3) and the tall, thin tower in the south-west corner (illus. 21). These tell us a great deal about the style and quality of his building and also contain evidence that the west wall, alongside the river, originally took a slightly different course. Excavation has also shed more light on how far his new castle transformed the site.

21. The south-west tower viewed from the castle courtyard

The 12th-Century Castle: The Courtyard Plan

A new fashion, especially favoured by the higher clergy, was to build castles with ordered and well-planned buildings surrounding a courtyard instead of the rather haphazard jumble which had tended to characterise castle *baileys* of the previous century. Some think this was inspired by the cloister arrangement used in monasteries. Alexander's own father had built two such castles, at Sherborne in Dorset and Old Sarum in Wiltshire, and Henry of Blois, Bishop of Winchester, was building another at Wolvesey, (Winchester) in Hampshire.

There would have been little point in superimposing Alexander's expensive stonework on an out-dated design and the excavated evidence seems to show that the entire site was levelled so that the castle plan could be re-modelled. The *ramparts* of the castle were reduced in height and the material spread around the *bailey* to create a flat, even platform for the new courtyard. So much material had been thrown down that the original *ramparts* must have stood very high. The amount also lends weight to the theory that a *motte* had been levelled, as this would have produced a great deal of soil. The flagged 11th-century courtyard was buried beneath

22. South section of Area 9, 1995. The slope seen in the clay marks the tail of the eastern rampart, which has been reduced in height and the soil thrown down to the right of it. The depth of the deposit can be seen in the wall of the cutting

3m. of redeposited clay (illus. 16). During excavations in 1995 the cutting in Area 9 clearly revealed the tail of the 11th-century *rampart* on the east side of the castle, the main part of which had been excavated in the 1950s by Barley and Waters. The tail shows as sloping lines on the extreme left of the *section* (side) of the cutting, with the clay which had been thrown down from the *ramparts* above and to the right of it (illus. 22).

23. Cobbled courtyard surface in Area 9

The cobbled courtyard of the redesigned castle came to light in Areas 7 and 9 and it had been resurfaced throughout its subsequent history (illus. 23).

The 12th-Century Castle: The Walls

Only short sections of the 12th-century *curtain walls* still stand. Two of these are on either side of the gatehouse (illus. 24). The largest is on the west side, where the outer face of the wall is intact almost to its original height of 20m. It was honeycombed with passages and *garderobes* (toilets) which stand revealed where the inner face of the wall has fallen away (illus. 25).

24. *The gatehouse with 12th-century curtain walls on either side. To the right of the photograph the change in the masonry shows where the north-west corner of the castle was extended towards the river during the early years of the 14th century. The north-west tower is on the extreme right*

The section of wall on the east side of the gatehouse was solid but only a short stub remains, standing almost to its full height (illus. 3 and 24). The doorway at the top, which can be seen in the photographs, led on to the *wall walk* from which guards could keep watch or defend the castle if necessary. An archaeological survey carried out in 1991 showed that this section of wall had been keyed into the main body of the gatehouse using a massive framework of timber. Horizontal beams which ran through the wall thickness at three levels had been jointed into others which lay in the thickness of the gatehouse wall. These frames were used to bind the heavy masonry structure together until the mortar had set firm, a process which could take up to a year. After this the frame's purpose had been served. It remained buried within the walls but the timber rotted away, leaving hollow rectangular channels. It was common practice in 12th-century castle building to build a gatehouse of stone first, leaving the defences in earth and timber to be converted later into stone as funds became available. It was considered important to make the gatehouse strong, as the entry was a weak point in the defences, but another consideration was that this building should make a good first impression, proclaiming the importance of the owner of the castle. The evidence for the timber frame at Newark proved beyond doubt that the gatehouse and the stone curtain walls were built at the same time, showing that no expense was spared when the castle was converted to stone.

Unlike the north-west section of wall, which forms a right angle with the gatehouse, the north-east section ran off at an acute outwards angle (illus. 14). It seems to have followed the line of defence laid out for the early Norman castle, for excavations in Area 3 indicated that the 11th-century *rampart* followed the same course. When *ramparts* were being constructed, they were built around timber upright posts which helped to stabilise the earth while it settled. Although the rampart had all but gone, a series of *post-holes* was found

25. The inner face of the 12th-century north curtain wall has fallen away, showing wall passages. There was a turret in the corner between the wall and the gatehouse which has also fallen. The vault of its chamber on the second floor can clearly be seen

following this line which probably show the direction it took (a group of these can be seen marked 390, 392, 420, 402, 396, 394, 428 and 355 on illus. 7). The reduced *rampart*, whose clay had became rock hard after 60 years of settlement, was used as the foundation of the wall, with only a single course of *Lias Limestone* set into it at an angle before the wall was built on top (illus. 26).

On the southern perimeter another stub of the curtain wall is still attached to the south-west tower (illus. 21). This too had passages in its thickness and one can see where the outer face of this wall was keyed into the south-west tower by following a line of *tusking stones* almost to the top. A passage was cut through when the wall was demolished and now appears as an arch at present ground level (on the left of illus. 21). The ground here was made up during the 18th century and this passage would have been on the first floor. Excavations in Area 8 concentrated on investigating the foundations of this wall and the area just in front of the tower. Again, the red clay *rampart* of the early castle was found to underlie the base of the 12th-century *curtain wall*, although here several courses of *Lias Limestone* had been set in *herring-bone* fashion as a foundation (illus. 27). The base of this *rampart* still slopes down to the southern ditch outside the castle and this was covered in a stone *revetment* so that it would not detract from the appearance of the new *curtain wall* placed on top of it. This can still be seen outside the castle beside the south-west tower if you walk down the landscaped gardens at Cuckstool Wharf (illus. 29).

The west *curtain wall*, which ran alongside the river, took a slightly different course from the ruined wall which stands today, for this was rebuilt around the turn of the 14th century on an altered alignment. Originally the wall adjoined the south-west tower, where a small amount of 12th-century fabric can be seen, but at the north end it formed a corner with the north *curtain wall* much nearer to the gatehouse, making a truer right angle (illus. 20). This corner is preserved in the stonework on the exterior face of the north curtain (illus. 28). Although this wall was demolished when the later wall was built, it may have had a *watergate* to the river. The remains of a staircase which led down from the courtyard area towards the river has a 12th-century *barrel vault*. Part of this survives in the *undercroft* under the present day terrace in the castle grounds (illus. 30). The staircase was blocked and the upper part buried. Excavations in Area 5 found the upper part of the staircase, although much of the stone from the steps had been *robbed out*, and dated the blocking to the late 15th or early 16th century .

The 12th-Century Castle: Excavated Buildings

Traces of three 12th-century buildings were found during the excavations. In Area 7 the base of a wall was preserved (illus. 31). It had no proper foundations, but the earlier *rampart* had been cut down here and the packed clay was set so hard the builders thought none necessary. There was a doorway which had been blocked and the building had later been cut short at its west end. The blocking contained 13th/14th-century pottery, so the alterations seem to have been carried out at a time when we know the castle was undergoing considerable change. A second building was found in Area 8 near the south-west tower. This too was built on

26. The base of the north-east section of the 12th-century curtain wall, with pitched Lias Limestone and rampart clay for a foundation

27. The foundations of the 12th-century south curtain wall set into the 11th century rampart

28. The north-west corner of the 12th-century castle. At the turn of the 14th century the north curtain was extended westwards towards the river

29. The base of the southern defences seen from Cuckstool Wharf. The slope is the base of the 11th-century rampart which was covered in stone during the 12th century

30. Stairs which linked the courtyard with the undercroft belong to an earlier date and might originally have led to a watergate in the 12th-century curtain wall. The blocking which can be seen was dated to the late 15th or early 16th century

rampart clay and was first built in timber, then replaced in stone. The levelling of the site which had been carried out to create the new castle had been done so accurately that the floor level of this building differed from floor levels in the gatehouse area by an average of only 8cm. Building materials recovered from the excavation included plaster, ceramic floor tiles, and roof tiles of both ceramic and stone.

In Area 3 a massive foundation trench came to light, marked 255 on illus. 7. Few features survived from the Norman period in this area, but the trench was so deep it intruded into the 10th-century and earlier layers. It was L-shaped and the longest leg, which carried on towards the south into ground which was not excavated, was 1.8m. wide. It had contained a stone wall, for there were a few *Lias Limestone* slabs set on edge in the bottom still in place, which were identical to foundation courses found elsewhere in 12th-century buildings on the site. Also there were mortar traces left in the side of the trench. It is likely that its foundations had been similar to those used on the gatehouse, which were also investigated. Here, three courses of *Lias Limestone* had been set into a deep trench, then a raft of large flat limestone slabs had been laid on top, over which the gatehouse walls were erected (illus. 32). The stone from trench 255 had been *robbed out* after the castle was demolished, for the trench contained pottery of the 17th to 18th centuries. The feature indicates a very substantial wall running north-south but was puzzling as there was no comparable wall found to the east, which would have represented the other side of a building, and the north leg of the foundation led nowhere. When it was found in 1993, it was thought to be a *curtain wall* which would have split the castle into two parts; an inner courtyard on the west side, with the best apartments, and an outer *bailey* on the east side, with stables and ancillary buildings. The first problem with this interpretation was that the inner or best *bailey* would have been very long and thin, but more problems were to come. In the two following seasons of excavation cuttings were made on the south side of the site where the other end of such a wall should have turned up, but none was found. Our present state of knowledge leaves the feature an enigma which seems likely to remain unsolved unless further excavation can take place.

The 12th-Century Castle: Standing Buildings
The South-West Tower

Although nicknamed 'King John's Tower', there is nothing to link this building with the king. He died within the castle in 1216, but there would have been far better apartments for him to occupy, and the legend that he died in this tower is probably a 19th-century invention.

The tower had four storeys and the three lower rooms were all covered by thick *barrel vaults*.

31. A 12th-century building in Area 7. Notice it has no regular foundations, relying on the hard-packed clay of the earlier rampart for stability

32. The foundations of the gatehouse, overlying a Saxon burial

The level of the original courtyard, which was established by the 1995 excavation, was lower than modern ground level because the ground was artificially raised between the 18th and 19th centuries. A doorway in the north wall of the tower, and now reached by descending some steps, came directly off the courtyard and led to a passage on the ground floor (illus. 20B). At the end of the passage there is a basement prison with a sheer drop into it. The thick *barrel vault* above it would prevent any noise from disturbing other residents of the tower.

The first floor of the tower, which is now at ground level, housed a bed-chamber which was reached by a passage in the thickness of the south curtain wall (on the left of illus. 21). We do not know how this passage was reached, but it might have been through the

building which was excavated in Area 8, which stood against the south *curtain*. The traces of a *garderobe* remain on the left side of the passage and part of its chute can be seen in the outer face of the wall (illus. 33). Measuring 2.5m by 5m. the room may be considered small by modern standards, but 12th-century bedrooms were not often large and, as they were unheated, perhaps more cosy for being small. The doorway which now leads into this room from the terrace was made in the 19th century. There was another, similar, chamber on the floor above, also with a *garderobe*. Like the room below, this too was reached by a passage higher up in the south *curtain wall*. The two bed-chambers in the tower had independent access so that two different guests could be accommodated without getting in each other's way. The staircase and doorway by which this room is now reached is relatively modern, dating from the 19th century.

The top floor of the tower was reached from the *wall-walk* of the *curtain wall*, so it is likely to have been a guardroom rather than a bed-chamber. The pattern of placing two chambers sandwiched between a basement prison and a top-floor guardroom seems to have been a common formula with a long history. The early 14th-century towers of the castle used the same plan and it is found in many other castles. The thick vaults between the floors would prevent any sound rising from the prison, while the wall tops were the natural vantage points from which to mount guard.

33. The south side of the south-west tower. The remains of a garderobe chute can be seen in the angle between the tower and the curtain wall

The Gatehouse

Bishop Alexander's gatehouse is one of the finest examples to survive from the early 12th century, (illus. 3 and 24). There would almost certainly have been another entrance on Castle Gate, now gone, to link the castle directly with the town. But visiting dignitaries would approach the castle by the entrance we can still see and it was designed to impress them with the wealth, power and importance of its owner.

34. A photograph of about 1890 showing the newly landscaped castle grounds. The bridge pit in front of the gatehouse can still be seen

The northern *moat* ran in front of the gatehouse, so it was reached by a bridge. This was probably made in two sections, with a stone *pier* somewhere near the centre of the *moat* to support it. The section nearest the gatehouse would have been removed if the castle suffered attack, but there was no accommodation for lifting gear, so it was probably not raised very frequently. There are *abutments* for the bridge on either side of the entry arch and just in front of this there was a sheer drop into the *moat*. This was filled in when the castle grounds were landscaped in the 1880s, so that people can walk through the gatehouse, but the bridge pit can be seen on a Victorian photograph taken in about 1890 (illus. 34). The existence of this deep pit until relatively recent times explains why the good, smooth *ashlar* limestone on the front of the gatehouse has largely remained in place. It was almost totally removed from the rear of the building by *stone robbers,* but this activity was clearly considered too dangerous at the front.

Apart from the removable bridge, the gatehouse was not well defended. It had large windows overlooking the approach to the castle and only one set of gates, even though there were three archways where gates could have been hung. It seems likely that there was another small *bailey* between the north wall of the castle and Beastmarket Hill, extending to the river bridge. This would have provided a further, outer, line of defence. Although this had gone by the late 16th century, people could remember it in the 1590s. Perhaps this was the *rampart* referred to in Henry I's charter to Alexander. The northern *moat* is particularly wide where it approaches the river and in the Middle Ages it would have been flooded, so perhaps it was also used as a fishpond.

Once over the gatehouse bridge, the visitor would have passed through a set of heavy timber gates which could be secured by a drawbar. These were manned by the porter who waited in a lodge built into the wall thickness on the west side of the gate-passage (illus. 35A and 38). Having no window, this was lit by a lamp which stood in a niche which still exists in the north wall. The porter's lodge had a *barrel-vaulted* roof but most of this and all but the north wall were blown out when the Parliamentarians destroyed the castle. Alexander's gatehouse has many points of similarity with one built by his father, Roger of Salisbury, at Sherborne castle in Dorset about ten years earlier. Here the arrangements for sheltering the porter are almost exactly the same.

The visitor would emerge into the courtyard of the castle, which would have been surrounded by buildings. The kitchen and chapel would probably have been free-standing: chapels had to be orientated to face east and kitchens were kept separate from other buildings because they often caught fire. There was a double *garderobe* off the courtyard in the thickness of the north *curtain wall* (illus. 35A). Its two chutes, along with one from another *garderobe* higher up, can be seen on the exterior of the north *curtain* (illus. 48). The *garderobe* had no door, but there was a dog-leg in the passage into it, so one could not see straight in from the courtyard.

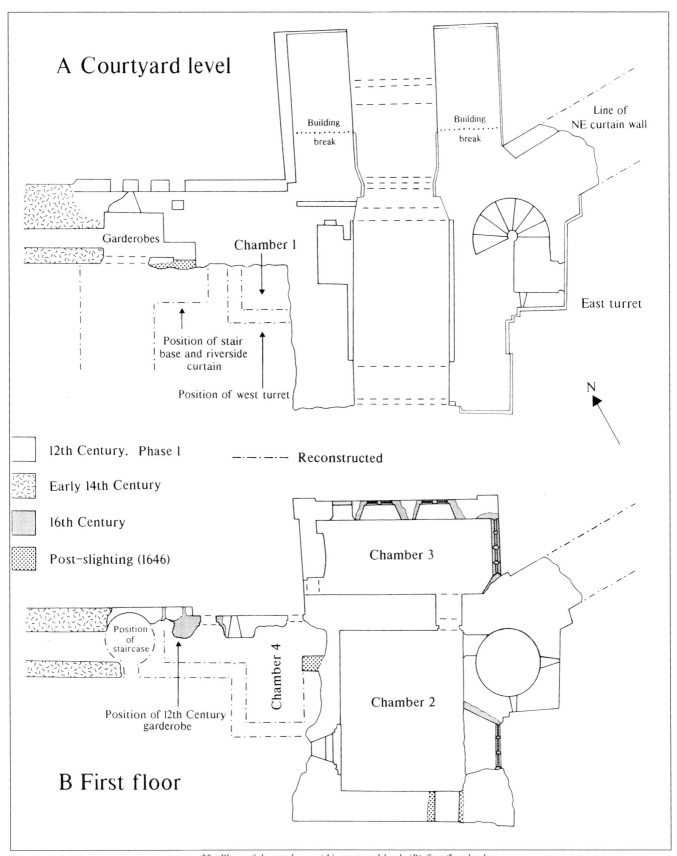

A Courtyard level

Building break

Building break

Line of NE curtain wall

Garderobes

Chamber 1

East turret

Position of stair base and riverside curtain

Position of west turret

N

12th Century. Phase 1 — · — · — Reconstructed

Early 14th Century

16th Century

Post-slighting (1646)

Chamber 3

Position of staircase

Chamber 4

Chamber 2

Position of 12th Century garderobe

B First floor

35. Plans of the gatehouse. (A) courtyard level. (B) first floor level

The top of this passage can still be seen in the north *curtain wall*, although it is now near ground level because the 12th-century courtyard lies at a depth of about 1.5m. The south wall of the *garderobe* was blown out when the castle was destroyed and is covered by a large grille (on the left of illus. 25).

36. The gatehouse (c.1930) looking north-west, showing the staircase turret

First Floor

Important visitors would no doubt have returned to the gatehouse (illus. 36) at some point, for the bishop had a special private suite on the first floor. It was entered by a doorway on the east side of the building which led to a spiral staircase housed in a turret rising to roof level (illus. 35 and 37). The stairs were very wide, allowing two people to walk abreast. They led to a large chamber (chamber 2) and from there one could enter a further chamber overlooking the approach to the castle (chamber 3). Because of alterations which took place during the late 16th and early 17th centuries, it is now difficult to determine the original function of these rooms. Chamber 2 has always been interpreted as a private chapel for the Bishop's use and it is drawn as such on the reconstruction of the gatehouse (illus. 38). If this was the case, chamber 3 seems to have been a private room beyond. It was very well-appointed with highly decorated windows (illus. 39 and 40). However, it is possible that chamber 2 was used as an audience chamber and that chamber 3 was the private chapel.

Beyond chamber 3 lay a bed-chamber (chamber 4), similar in size to those in the south-west tower, and with a private *garderobe* (illus. 35B and 37). The *garderobe* was at the end of a passage in the thickness of the north-west *curtain wall*. To get to it one stepped out of chamber 3 on to a timber gallery, then turned left through another door into the passage. These two adjacent doors can be seen from the northern *moat* and the joist-holes for the gallery still exist (illus. 42). They were used to reconstruct what it must have looked like (illus. 43). Despite the *moat* below, the gallery would have been something of a security risk without any further defences. It helps strengthen the argument that Alexander's castle had another *bailey* between here and Beast Market Hill.

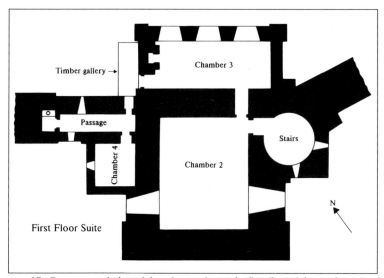
37. Reconstructed plan of the private suite on the first floor of the gatehouse

38. Reconstruction of the gatehouse c. 1140 with cutaway to show the interior

The bedroom (chamber 4) was in a turret attached to the west side of the gatehouse, which originally matched the staircase turret on the east side. Although the western turret has completely fallen down, you can see where it was attached to the gatehouse by the vertical row of *tusking stones* on its west wall. The turret has been reconstructed in illus. 44. Chamber 4 had a *barrel-vaulted* ceiling, part of which can still be seen (illus. 25).

Second Floor

When the gatehouse was first built there was no second floor in the main part. At this time chamber 2 rose through two storeys to the roof, but chamber 3 was only one storey tall, and had a roof which leaned against the front of the gatehouse (illus. 39). The diagonal line of its roof *crease* can still be seen on the end walls of chamber 3 (illus. 40). Originally, only the west turret had a room at second floor level (chamber 5 on illus.

41A). This room was ventilated by a window in the gatehouse front marked by diagonal dotted lines on illus. 41B. In the second half of the 12th century an extra room was built above chamber 3 (chamber 6 on illus. 41A) and the window was blocked at this time (illus. 45). A doorway into room 6 was cut through the *spine wall* of the gatehouse so that the new chamber could be reached from the east turret stairs (illus. 41A).

Although chamber 5 was housed in the top floor of the west turret, its access was not through the gatehouse. It was approached by a passage in the thickness of the north-west *curtain wall* at second floor level. This passage was reached by a spiral staircase at its east end (illus. 41A), but this only descended as far as the first floor (illus. 35B). Originally, it seems to have been reached at this level from the 12th-century west *curtain wall*, in much the same way that the south *curtain wall* was used to enter the south-west tower. When the west *curtain wall* was demolished and rebuilt nearer the river, the staircase was linked with a corridor in

39. Reconstruction of chamber 3

the new part of the wall (illus. 35B). As with the south-west tower, the two chambers in the west turret were approached by different means. The special suite on the first floor was in no way disturbed by other traffic, and its one means of entry, via the east turret, kept it more exclusive, more easily guarded and secure.

The Wall-Walks

The east turret stairs continued to roof level, where there were two doorways (illus. 41B). One led on to the wall walk of the north-east *curtain wall* (illus. 3 and 24), the other led on to the gutters of the gatehouse roof, and from there to the wall-walk of the north-west *curtain wall*. We also have evidence for a wall-walk on the south *curtain*, so it might have been possible for guards to complete a tour of the walls at this level. The east turret culminated in a look-out tower on the roof of the gatehouse (illus. 36). This is very ruined and much of what is left of it is covered in Victorian restoration, but vestiges of its stairs still exist. The east turret stairs served two very different purposes: to give access to the wall-walks as well as to the special gatehouse suite. Housing for a door was built into the staircase just above first floor level, so that the suite could be kept more private, and it would also have reduced the draughts which must have swept down from above.

40. View of chamber 3. Although the windows were blocked and replaced in the 16th century, some of the 12th-century decoration has survived on the original openings

26

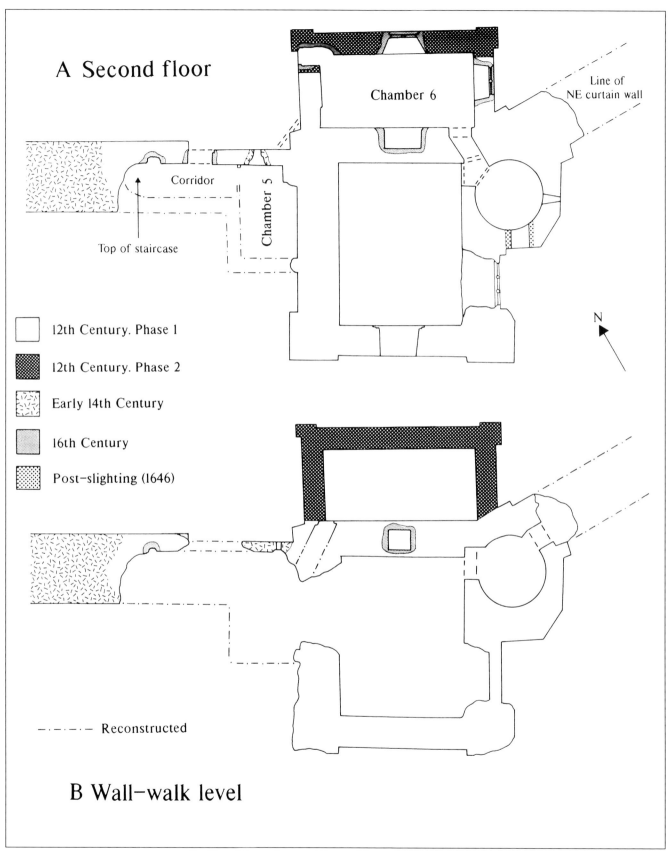

A Second floor

Chamber 6

Line of
NE curtain wall

Corridor

Chamber 5

Top of staircase

N

12th Century. Phase 1

12th Century. Phase 2

Early 14th Century

16th Century

Post–slighting (1646)

– · – · – Reconstructed

B Wall–walk level

41. Plan of the gatehouse at (A) second floor and (B) wall-walk levels

42. *The angle between the gatehouse and the north curtain wall. At first floor level this was bridged by a timber gallery.*
The joist-holes for the gallery are plainly visible

43. Reconstruction of the timber gallery at first floor level in the angle between the gatehouse and the north curtain wall

44. *Reconstruction of the west turret attached to the gatehouse. The ground floor was entered from the courtyard and might have been a guard room. The room above is chamber 4 and chamber 5 is on the top floor*

45. *Early 12th-century window opening in the front of the gatehouse, with wall of chamber 6 blocking it*

4. King John at Newark Castle

King John visited Newark Castle a number of times, his first visit occurring in 1205. The following year, as part of his power struggle with the Pope, John had taken control of the bishop's castle at Newark. Ten years later as civil war raged between the king and his discontented barons, Newark Castle was entrusted to one of his mercenaries, Robert de Gaugy. Already King John had demonstrated his military abilities and many of the rebel barons chose to make peace. In September 1216 he marched northwards, driving back the King of Scotland who had invaded as far as Cambridge, and relieved the siege of Lincoln by the rebel earl of the county. From there he travelled to Lynn where he was welcomed by the townspeople but contracted dysentery, perhaps exacerbated by over-indulgence at the festivities combined with fatigue. Leaving on 11th October he went to Wisbech and then Swineshead Abbey and during this journey occurred the legendary mishap of losing his baggage. According to the chronicler, Roger of Wendhover, *'the ground opened in the midst of the waters and whirlpools sucked in everything, men and horses'*. Precisely where this happened, what was lost and even if the king was present, is unknown. But he arrived at Swineshead Abbey sick, distressed and barely able to sit on his horse. Said to have worsened his condition by an over-indulgence in pears and new cider, he struggled on to Sleaford and then Newark Castle. Here, tended by the Abbot of Croxton who was known for his medical skill, the king lay dying for 3 days.

Letters came from a number of rebels wishing to make their peace, while King John dictated his will and on 18th October he died after the Abbot of Croxton heard his confession and performed the last rites. His intestines were taken away by the Abbot and, following his wishes, a funeral procession of soldiers carried the body to Worcester cathedral for burial (illus. 46).

John's eldest son Henry, only 9 years old, was crowned King but Newark Castle's role was not yet over. The following year Robert de Gaugy was ordered by the new King, Henry III, on the advice of his regent William Marshall, to give up the castle to the Bishop of Lincoln. Despite several forceful reminders, Robert de Gaugy refused and in 1218 the castle was besieged by a strong force. The strength of the castle's defences is shown in that, although stone-throwing engines were used as well as men with pick axes, even after a week they had failed to take the castle. Instead, after negotiations, Robert de Gaugy agreed to leave the castle for £100 of silver to compensate for the provisions he would leave behind. According to the Annals of Dunstable he did not have long to enjoy his gains:

'In the same year (1218) Robert de Gaugy was excommunicated because he would not surrender the Castle of Newark, and because he had devastated the surrounding country; but after a time he unwillingly restored the Castle, and the same year died at St. Neots, "Smitten with the infernal fire".'

46. Drawing of King John's tomb in Worcester Cathedral by William Stukeley (published 1776)

31

5. The Early 14th-Century Castle

About the turn of the 14th century the castle was again remodelled. A town *watergate* might have been built outside the south-west tower at Cuckstool Wharf, as the foundations of a stone tower came to light there in 1984 (illus. 47). The west curtain wall of the castle was torn down and rebuilt with its north end nearer to the river, making an acute angle in the north-west corner (illus. 20). The alteration is best seen on the exterior face of the north *curtain wall* (illus. 24 and 42), where there is a marked difference in the masonry between the 12th-century work to the east (left) and the smoother 14th century work to the west (right). A drawing of the elevation makes the change even clearer (illus. 48). The lower part of the corner of the 12th-century castle is still preserved (illus. 29, 42 and 48).

There were two motives for altering the course of the wall. In the first place, by pushing the corner out by about 9m. a considerably larger area was enclosed. It made possible the building of a whole new range of accommodation against the rebuilt *curtain wall*. These buildings fitted and worked together in a complicated plan and it was certainly easier to achieve this by building anew rather than try to convert existing buildings. Secondly, the new wall with its range of buildings was to be in the latest style. Once again, Newark castle was to have 'state of the art' architecture with, apparently, no cost spared.

The exterior of the river curtain was faced in smooth *ashlar,* using two different coloured stones: limestone and sandstone (see photograph on the front cover). The new wall had two towers, one in the north-west corner and another placed in the centre (illus. 20). These were neither square nor round, but *polygonal:* the central tower forms a half hexagon and the north-west tower is pentagonal. This was

47. *Foundations of a stone tower found at Cuckstool Wharf during excavations in 1984*

all done deliberately for effect. Both *polychrome* masonry and *polygonal* towers appeared on Edward I's new castle at Caernarvon, designed by James of St. George, a master builder brought from Savoy to carry out the king's architectural ambitions. Begun in 1283, this castle was designed to act as the seat of Edward's newly-established government in North Wales. Its constable was to be regarded as the king's viceroy and the very building sent out architectural messages. The multi-coloured masonry was copied from the walls of Theodosius in Constantinople and symbolised imperial status, while *polygonal* towers were reserved for palaces. Edward I might have used Caernarvon castle as a means of intimidating the Welsh, but he also set a fashion. Clearly the Bishop of Lincoln wished to proclaim that his castle at Newark was a palace too. No document tells us which bishop started the work. An inquest of 1284 states that *'Walter de Neweport, mason, in the castle of Newark, fell from a certain beam in the turret, and forthwith died.'* Was he working on the rebuild or simply doing running repairs? The work may have been set in train by Bishop Oliver Sutton (1280-1300), although it would have been finished by his successors. We know Sutton was military-minded because he fortified the cathedral close at Lincoln. Also that he was actively looking into his property at Newark, as he reclaimed land from people whose title deeds he found defective. Perhaps it is significant that Anthony Bek, Bishop of Durham, had recently built a new castle at Somerton in Lincolnshire, on Sutton's 'patch': the possibility of one-upmanship cannot be ruled out.

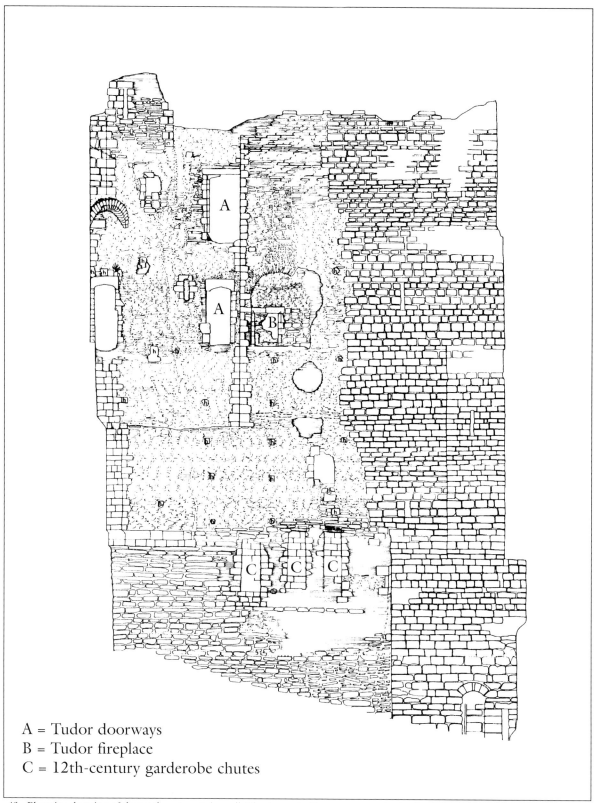

A = Tudor doorways
B = Tudor fireplace
C = 12th-century garderobe chutes

48. Elevation drawing of the north-west curtain wall. The change in the masonry can be clearly seen and the straight vertical line near the bottom marks the corner of the 12th-century castle. Two doors, one above the other high in the wall were added in the 16th century when a timber-framed extension was jettied out of the wall here. It was two storeys high and the lower room had a fireplace (to the right of the lower door). In the centre of the elevation, towards the bottom, the three chutes from the 12th-century garderobes can be seen

The Halls

There was a long range of buildings set against the new *curtain wall*. Although the buildings themselves have mostly gone, we can tell a great deal about them from evidence left in the wall. Their great windows are still there: the west front of the castle was so well protected by the river that large windows here were no risk to security. The *crease* of the buildings' roof can still be seen in the face of the north *curtain* where it was extended to meet the new west wall, and some of the doorways still exist. One led from the top floor of the north-west tower on to the roof gutter and would have been used for maintenance as well as access to the *wall-walk* (illus. 49).

In castles of the time it was common to have a large *hall,* which could be used to conduct business and double as a communal dining hall, with more private rooms at one end. *Halls* were not yet provided with fireplaces, but a hearth would be set in the floor in the centre of the room and the smoke found its way out through a *louvre* in the roof. This was one reason why *halls* had no ceilings but were open to the rafters, and were very tall, the equivalent of two storeys high. The private rooms were called chambers and these were often divided into two floors. At Newark there were two *halls* set end to end, each with two very large windows and each with a two-storey set of chambers at one end (illus. 50). The northern *hall* was probably used by the bishop and his household, with his chambers in the north-west corner (illus. 51). He would retire to these for private meetings, perhaps with his more honoured guests. Beyond the chamber block, rooms became smaller and ever more private. A doorway from the lower chamber led into the north-west tower (where the modern door into the tower is now). There were two private chambers with *garderobes* in the tower, where the bishop probably slept. Another doorway from the upper chamber can be seen half way up the wall on illus. 49. It led to a corridor which connected with the spiral staircase to chamber 5 (illus. 35B and 41A).

The southern *hall*, (illus. 50 and 51), was perhaps used more for business, although it would also have been used for dining, particularly if a guest arrived with a very large retinue of followers. It too had two floors of chambers at its south end. The window of the upper chamber was divided into two lights, and can be seen high in the west *curtain wall*. The doorway to the left of it leads into a *garderobe*, which was built in the wall thickness, with a chute discharging straight into the river.

During the 1993 excavations there was an opportunity to investigate the inner wall of the *halls* range. A small cutting was made in Area 4 (illus. 6), which uncovered the east wall of the range (illus. 52). Although the foundation was of stone, it was not substantial enough to have supported a stone wall, so the inner walls of the halls were *timber-framed* (illus. 51). Other *timber-framed* buildings of the same date were found by excavation in Areas 7, 8 and 9. Area 7 produced a large amount of kitchen waste from this period and, although the kitchen building was not discovered, it could not have been far away. The 12th-century courtyard was resurfaced several times, *jettons* of the reign of Edward I or II helping to date some of these.

Towers and Prisons

The north-west tower (illus. 2) followed the same formula as the 12th-century south-west tower in having a prison in the basement, a chamber on each of the two middle floors, and a guard-room on the top floor. The prison (illus. 20B) is shaped like a bee-hive, with a *corbelled vault*. Prisoners were thrown in from a trapdoor high in its shoulder. When the north *curtain wall* was extended, a corridor was made to run westwards from the 12th-century *garderobe* (illus. 35A and 20A) and this descends by steps towards the *oubliettes*. Apart from the round prison in the tower, there is a square one next door in the base of the west *curtain wall* (illus. 20B). Each has a single narrow window, barely enough to let in air. The entrances to these prisons were so high that prisoners could not hope to reach them, yet the trap-doors were fitted with drawbars to make sure they did not escape. Probably injured on entry, they would have to rely on friends to bring them food. In 1476 a glover, William Spondon, left 20 shillings (£1) in his will for the comfort of convicted prisoners in the castle dungeon.

The tower in the centre of the west *curtain wall* had two more prisons, making a total of five in the castle that we know about. The tower has lost its east wall (illus. 53). When this was in place, it would have formed the middle of the south *hall*, with a window on either side (illus. 50). It was through the side of the right

49. Looking towards the north-west corner of the halls range. The crease of the roof is clearly visible. The doorway to its left led on to the roof gutters and would have been used for maintenance. The doorway in the centre of the wall led out of the bishop's upper chamber

hand window that one reached the central tower (illus. 50 and 20A). Passing the spiral staircase to the upper floors, one descended a few steps to a doorway which was barred against the room, indicating that whoever was inside was shut in. However this was a much more comfortable jail than the *oubliettes*, of which there was another beneath, reached by a trapdoor in the floor (illus. 20B).

The first room reached by the stairs was a bed-chamber, with a *garderobe* in the wall thickness to the south. The upper room has been so refaced it is difficult to determine its function. It might have been another chamber, or a guardroom. There can be no doubt that the late 13th/early 14th-century phase at Newark was strongly influenced by Edward I's new castles in Wales. There are several similarities between the central tower at Newark and the Prison Tower in Conway castle, north Wales, built, like Caernarvon, by Edward I. Both are entered from the *hall* by an opening in the side of a window recess. Both have an *oubliette* surmounted by a less savage prison. Both have a chamber with *garderobe* on the floor above and a further chamber over that. The direct access from prison to *hall* suggests that the southern *hall* might have been routinely used as the manor court, and it has been reconstructed as such in illus. 51. Perhaps the jailer occupied the bedchamber in the central tower.

The Undercroft

In the 12th century the riverside *curtain wall* would have stood on top of the river cliff. When the new *curtain wall* replaced it, it was built at the bottom of the cliff. This left enough space to build the two *oubliettes* at the north end (under and beside the north-west tower) at riverbank level (illus. 20B). There was some space left further south and, with some further excavation into the cliff, this was used to build an *undercroft*, or vaulted cellar, underneath the bishop's *hall* (illus. 55). A *watergate* on the riverbank was built into the *curtain wall* so

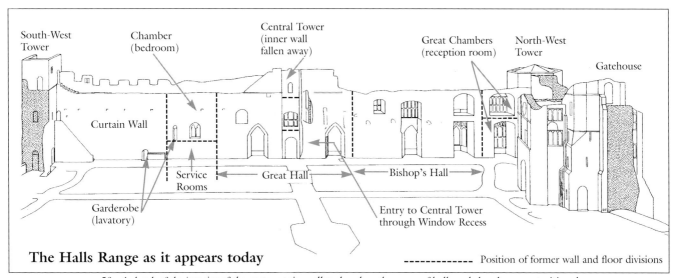

South-West Tower · Chamber (bedroom) · Central Tower (inner wall fallen away) · Great Chambers (reception room) · North-West Tower · Gatehouse

Curtain Wall · Service Rooms · Great Hall · Bishop's Hall · Garderobe (lavatory) · Entry to Central Tower through Window Recess

The Halls Range as it appears today

------------- Position of former wall and floor divisions

50. A sketch of the interior of the west curtain wall to show how the range of halls and chambers were positioned

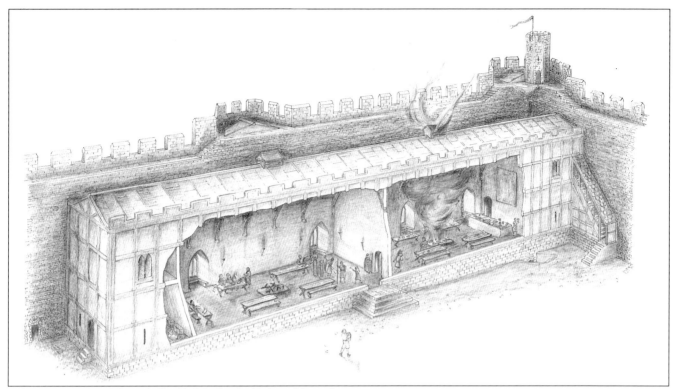

51. Reconstruction of the two halls with their chamber blocks at either end. The southern hall is being used to conduct a court, while the northern hall is prepared for a meal

that goods could be conveniently delivered by boat (illus. 54). A passageway then led up towards the *undercroft* where the goods were stored in cool, dark, but well-ventilated conditions (illus. 20B, 56 and 57). The west front of the castle was well defended because of the river, so the *watergate* would not be much of a weak point. But just in case, its heavy door was well barred and the entry was protected by a *meurtriere*. At the top of the *watergate* stairs a narrow chamber between the passage and the store-room might have been used by a clerk to keep account of what came in and out. The whole complex is characterised by typical late 13th/early 14th-century building style except the staircase which led up to the courtyard (illus. 30). Its *barrel vault* is typical of the 12th-century work and even the mortar in the joints matches the older parts of the castle: it may represent an earlier *watergate* to the river. When it was blocked, towards the end of the 15th century, another entrance was made in the south wall of the *undercroft* (illus. 20B), but this is now dangerous and rarely used.

52. The foundation of the east wall of the hall range, excavated in 1993

6. The Castle in the 15th, 16th and early 17th Centuries

53. The central tower in the river curtain. The nearest, east wall has fallen away and the spiral staircase on the right, which led to the upper floors, is also revealed

In the late Middle Ages the owners of the castle, which had always been as much a palace as a fortification, became more and more concerned with comfort. Fireplaces were put into the two chambers in the north-west tower (illus. 58). Window glass became cheaper and more commonly used and the lead from glazed windows was a common find during the excavations. Bishop Thomas Rotherham (1471-1480) replaced the windows in the south-west tower, his chamber block and at the north end of his *hall* (illus. 59). Documentary sources suggest that the east ditch of the castle was silting up – it was let for grazing in 1435 for 10 shillings (50p) a year. The 1992 excavation in Area 1 (illus. 6) showed that the northern ditch must have silted by the early 17th century, when it was re-cut in an effort to refortify the castle during the Civil War sieges of Newark.

54. Reconstruction of the riverside curtain wall in the 15th century

55. The undercroft at Newark Castle in the early 19th century

Rotherham was the last cleric to leave his mark on the castle, for it reverted to the Crown at the *Reformation*. Falling slowly into decay, it was brought into service in 1536 when the *Pilgrimage of Grace* threatened civil unrest in the East Midlands. Complaints were sent to the king that the castle had '*scant lodging for 100 men and no water*'. From 1560 the castle was leased to Sir Francis Leeke, who seems to have done little to it. It was not until the Earl of Rutland took the lease in 1581, at a peppercorn rent on condition he improved it, that any repairs were carried out. He got permission to demolish a tower in order to use the materials. After the earl's death, the castle passed to his widow and then to their son-in-law, Lord Burghley, who spent £400 in 1607 when the castle '*was repaired in stone, wood, iron, glass, lead and tile.*'

The Tudor and Stuart alterations were primarily concerned with providing more rooms. The *halls* were cut horizontally into two floors, with new windows inserted at the higher level, as was chamber 2 in the gatehouse. Most of the 12th-century gatehouse windows were blocked and replaced with more fashionable models (illus. 36, 40 and 60). Extra fireplaces were also put in. Chamber 6 had one added and there may have been another high in the wall of the southern hall, although it was refaced with paving stone in the 19th century (illus. 53).

Perhaps the most bizarre alteration took place in the angle between the north *curtain wall* and the front of the gatehouse (illus. 42): it demonstrates how keen the owners were at the time to increase the number of rooms. The timber gallery (illus. 43) was removed and replaced by a two-storeyed *timber-framed* extension *jettied* out from the castle walls. Doors into the new rooms were created, one from the first floor corridor and the other from the top floor corridor (illus. 48). The lower room had a fireplace whose flue was built where the old *garderobe* had been on the first floor and the hearth blocked the 12th-century *garderobe* chute (illus. 35B).

Lord Burghley's improvements seem to have had the desired effect; the castle became a comfortable country house. In 1603 the new king, James I, stayed there on his way from Scotland to London and repeated visits by his son, Charles I, show that the building remained in good repair throughout the early 17th century. Its popularity with the king might have contributed to its destruction in 1646.

56. The watergate passage

57. The undercroft

It is well known that the town of Newark held out for the Royalist cause during the Civil War (1642-6) until ordered to surrender by the king, who had given himself up to the Scots Army. Unfortunately little was recorded about the castle during this time, although it would have had a significant role. It was garrisoned and several men were killed on the *ramparts* by Parliamentary fire. Nor is it known what measures were taken to refortify it except for the re-cutting of the north castle ditch, found in the excavation of Area 1 in 1992. After the surrender, the townsfolk and local villagers were ordered to demolish all of the siege works, including the castle.

58. The second floor chamber of the north-west tower. Note the fireplace stands high in the wall because the floor was replaced by 18th-century squatters at a different level from the original

59. Oriel window placed in the bishop's hall, late 15th century

39

7. 1646 and After

When Parliament ordered the destruction of the castle, a great opportunity arose for salvaging the building materials. Some of the *timber-framed* buildings might have been dismantled and taken away. The stone buildings were made unusable by blowing them up with gunpowder. Judging from the damage inflicted, we can guess that one barrel was placed in the porter's lodge on the west side of the gate passage and another was put in the corridor on the first floor in the thickness of the north-west *curtain wall*, but there would have been many more. One man was accidentally killed during the operation. Although the buildings were put out of action it is likely that the bulk of the castle still stood, but after it was abandoned it became fair game for *stone robbers*. Many of the town houses must incorporate castle stone and it may be significant that the remaining ruins are farthest away from the town.

Some decided it was easier to move into the ruins. The north-west tower was occupied by squatters who put in new floors at different levels from the originals (illus. 58). A print of 1790 shows a dormer roof sticking out of the upper chamber window in the tower (illus. 61). By the early 19th century people had placed cottages against the inside of the river curtain and one person was living in Bishop Rotherham's *oriel* window. The castle had become something of a slum and there was a coal wharf on the river bank beside the north-west tower (illus. 15). In 1839 the tenements which had grown up beside the gatehouse were cleared and the area became a cattle market (illus. 1).

60. Elevation drawing of the front of the gatehouse. The outline of the round-headed 12th-century windows can be seen: they were blocked and replaced in the late 16th or early 17th century by square-headed openings

Yet despite its sorry state, interest in the castle as an historic building was beginning to be kindled. The Crown had acquired the manor of Newark in 1547 but sold off the bulk of its Newark holdings in 1836. However, it retained the castle and between 1845-8 it became the first historic monument to be consolidated at government expense: £650 was spent on restoration work. The architect Anthony Salvin, who had a reputation for restoring historic monuments, was appointed and he reported that the gatehouse was filled with earth almost to the springing of the arches and that its foundations had been eroded. Salvin's restoration was sensitive to the building and of such high quality that in parts it is now difficult to tell his work from the original. He also designed a public bath-house which was built in the south-east corner of the castle grounds but has since been demolished.

In 1887 the Town Corporation set in motion plans to remove the cattle market and landscape the site as a public park, which opened in 1889 (illus. 34 and 62). The ruins were seen as a rather romantic back-drop to this exercise and it is likely that a great deal of surviving castle fabric was carted away. Whatever might have been left of the *halls* range was levelled and a tarmac terrace was laid over the *undercroft*. The ruins received

61. Print of 1790 by D. Martin while the castle was occupied by squatters

another campaign of consolidation, but this time much less sensitive than that of the 1840s. Wall tops were capped with concrete and tarmac and the walls were refaced in York paving stone, most of which is still in place and can be clearly seen in patches all over the fabric (illus. 53).

In the late 1980s and early 1990s the castle was consolidated again. The north-west tower was given a new roof and the wall tops covered in Blue Lias Limestone, which can easily be identified from original castle masonry. The park continues to be a pleasant amenity for the people of Newark and visitors, with summer events, such as concerts, a further attraction.

The interest shown by Newark residents in the 1992-5 seasons of excavations proved that the story of Newark castle still commands their curiosity and affection.

62. The park c. 1890

Glossary

abutments	Short projecting walls to support a bridge.
angle tower	A tower placed at the corners or angles of the castle enclosure.
ashlar	Good quality building stone which has a smooth face.
bailey	An open area enclosed by castle defences containing buildings. Castles sometimes had more than one bailey.
barrel vault	A stone ceiling shaped like a half barrel.
cist	A box made of stone slabs, often used in graves.
corbelled vault	A round stone ceiling made by having each course of masonry reduce in circumference so that the ceiling becomes narrower as it gets taller, like a bee hive.
crease	The mark left on a wall where a roof has been removed: often made by a row of projecting stones where the lead flashing was attached.
curtain wall	A main wall that enclosed and protected a castle.
garderobe	A medieval toilet: often a hole over a chute built into a wall so that waste would be carried outside the building.
grave goods	Objects buried with a corpse for use in the after life. The practice was not followed by Christians.
hall	The principal room in a medieval house which was used for communal meals and to conduct business: in a castle it was often a separate building.
herring-bone	Laying stones upright so that one course leans diagonally one way and the next course leans in the opposite direction.
jettied	The practice of building the upper storey of a timber-framed building so that it projected beyond the lower storey.
jetton	A counter used in the Middle Ages to do sums.
lias limestone	A type of limestone used for building.
loom-weights	Round weights with holes in the middle, rather like pottery doughnuts, which were tied to the warp threads on a primitive loom to keep them taut.
louvre	A structure which was built on the roof of a building where there was an open hearth. The louvre had a roof on it to keep out the rain, but had holes in the sides to let out the smoke
meurtriere	A hole in a ceiling through which missiles could be dropped on to attackers.
moat	A ditch which was used to defend a castle. Not usually filled with water, although some were.
motte	An artificial hill shaped like an upturned pudding basin on which was built a stockade and tower, usually in timber.
oriel	A projecting window.
oubliette	From the French 'to forget': a prison or dungeon made in a cellar with access by a trap door, usually in the ceiling. Occasionally made in the shape of a bottle and called a 'bottle prison'.

palisade	A defensive wall made of a row of timber stakes.
pier	A stone support, often like a very thick column.
Pilgrimage of Grace	A popular uprising against the king in 1536. It had many causes, one of which was objection to closing the monasteries.
polychrome	Multi-coloured.
polygonal	Having many sides and angles.
post-holes	A hole dug into the ground to support an upright post. When the timber of the post rots away, archaeological evidence for the hole remains.
radio carbon dating	A scientific method of dating organic archaeological finds, like bones, by measuring the levels of carbon 14 in the material.
rampart	An earth bank which was thrown up to defend an enclosure.
Reformation	The movement towards religious change in the early 16th century which culminated in the English king becoming head of the church in England in 1534, rather than the Pope.
revetment	A wall of stone or timber which stops an earth bank from collapsing.
robbed out	Where stone has been taken from an abandoned building.
section	The straight side of an archaeological cutting in which different soil layers can be seen.
spine wall	The central wall across the middle of a large square building.
stone robbers	People who remove stone from an abandoned building.
timber-framed	A method of building where the skeleton of the building is formed by timbers jointed together, then the walls filled in with another material, often wattle and daub plastered over.
tusking stones	Stones which are deliberately left sticking out of a wall so that another wall can be keyed into it.
undercroft	A vaulted cellar in the basement of a building.
wall walk	A walkway along the top of a curtain wall from which a lookout could be kept: also used when fighting off attackers.
watching brief	The practice of having professional archaeologists watch where work is being carried out below ground in places where archaeological features are likely to show up. They are then recorded by notes, drawings and photographs.
watergate	A doorway or gate in a castle or town defences which gave access to a river.

Further Reading

Barley M & Waters F	1956	'Newark Castle Excavations', *Trans. Thoroton Society* **60**, 20-33
Blagg T	1906	Guide to Newark Castle
Braun H	1935	'Notes on Newark Castle', *Trans. Thoroton Society* **39**, 53-91
Brown C	1904-1907	History of Newark Vol I and Vol II
Brown R Allen	1970	English Castles
Cathcart King DJ	1988	The Castle in England and Wales: An Interpretative History
Coupland F, Marshall P & Samuels J	1994	Newark Castle Studies: Excavations 1994
Courtney T W	1973	'Newark Castle Excavations 1972', *Trans. Thoroton Society* **77**, 34-40
Dickinson W	1816	History and Antiquities of the town of Newark
Dixon P, Marshall P Palmer-Brown C & Samuels J	1994	Newark Castle Studies : Excavations 1992-1993
Kenyon J G	1991	Medieval Fortifications
Kinsley A G	1989	*The Anglo-Saxon Cemetery at Millgate, Newark-on-Trent, Nottinghamshire.* Nottinghamshire Archaeological Monographs No 2
Kinsley A G	1993	'Excavations of the Saxo-Norman Town defences at Slaughterhouse Lane, Newark-on-Trent, Nottinghamshire', *Trans. Thoroton Society* **98**, 14-63
Marshall P	forthcoming	'A Survey of the Romanesque Gatehouse at Newark Castle, Nottinghamshire', *Archaeological Journal*
Marshall P	1997	'The 12th-Century Castle at Newark, Nottinghamshire', *Trans. of the British Archaeological Association: Southwell and the Buildings of Nottinghamshire*
Marshall P & Samuels J	1994	'Recent Excavation at Newark Castle, Nottinghamshire', *Trans. Thoroton Society* **98**, 49-57
Platt C	1982	The Castle in Medieval England and Wales
Pounds N J G	1990	The Medieval Castle in England and Wales
Rogers A	1974	'The Origins of Newark : The Evidence of Local Boundaries', *Trans. Thoroton Society* **78**, 13-26
Thompson M W	1987	The Decline of the Castle
Thompson M W	1991	The Rise of the Castle
Todd M	1974	'Excavations on the Medieval Defences of Newark, 1972', *Trans. Thoroton Society*, **78**, 27-53
Todd M	1977	'Excavations on the Medieval defences of Newark, 1976', *Trans. Thoroton Society*, **81**, 42-8
Trollope E	1871	'Newark Castle', *Reports and Papers of the Lincoln Diocesan Architectural Society*, 50-7